Dinosaur Warriors

by Ruth Owen

Consultant:
Dougal Dixon, Paleontologist
Member of the Society of Vertebrate Paleontology
United Kingdom

BEARPORT
PUBLISHING

New York, New York

Credits

Cover, © James Kuether; 4–5, © James Kuether; 6–7, © James Kuether; 8, © The Natural History Museum/Alamy; 9, © James Kuether; 10–11, © James Kuether; 10B, © Christophe Hendrickx; 12–13, © James Kuether; 14, © The Natural History Museum/Alamy; 15, © James Kuether; 16, © David A. Burnham; 17, © John Weinstein/Field Museum/Getty Images; 18, © James Kuether; 19, © Andrey Gudkov/Dreamstime; 20, © Gaston Design Inc./Robert Gaston/www.gastondesign.com; 21, © Stocktrek Images Inc/Alamy; 22T, © W. Scott McFill/Shutterstock; 22B, © James Kuether; 23T, © Edward Ionescu/Dreamstime; 23B, © benedek/Istock Photo.

Publisher: Kenn Goin
Senior Editor: Joyce Tavolacci
Creative Director: Spencer Brinker
Image Researcher: Ruth Owen Books

Library of Congress Cataloging-in-Publication Data

Names: Owen, Ruth, 1967– author.
Title: Dinosaur warriors / by Ruth Owen.
Description: New York, New York : Bearport Publishing, [2019] | Series: The
    dino-sphere | Includes bibliographical references
    and index.
Identifiers: LCCN 2018049812 (print) | LCCN 2018053176 (ebook) | ISBN
    9781642802566 (Ebook) | ISBN 9781642801873 (library)
Subjects: LCSH: Dinosaurs—Juvenile literature.
Classification: LCC QE861.5 (ebook) | LCC QE861.5 .O8456 2019 (print) | DDC
    567.9—dc23
LC record available at https://lccn.loc.gov/2018049812

For more information, write to Bearport Publishing Company, Inc., 45 West 21st Street, Suite 3B, New York, New York 10010. Printed in the United States of America.

10 9 8 7 6 5 4 3 2 1

Contents

Time to Fight!

There's a big cloud of dirt.

A male *Triceratops* charges at a bigger male.

Behind them is a **herd** of females.

The smaller male wants to lead the herd!

A *Triceratops* had a big, colorful neck frill. Males probably shook the frills to show their strength.

neck frill

Triceratops
(try-SER-uh-tops)

5

Who's the Strongest?

Crash! The two *Triceratops* warriors lock horns.

Each one tries to push the other away from the herd.

The winner of the battle will lead the group!

Triceratops was a plant-eating dinosaur. Its name means "three-horned head."

Horns for Fighting

How do we know *Triceratops* used its horns for fighting?

Scientists have found **fossils** of *Triceratops* skulls.

The skulls have holes in them.

The holes were made by the horns of other *Triceratops*!

Triceratops **horn fossil**

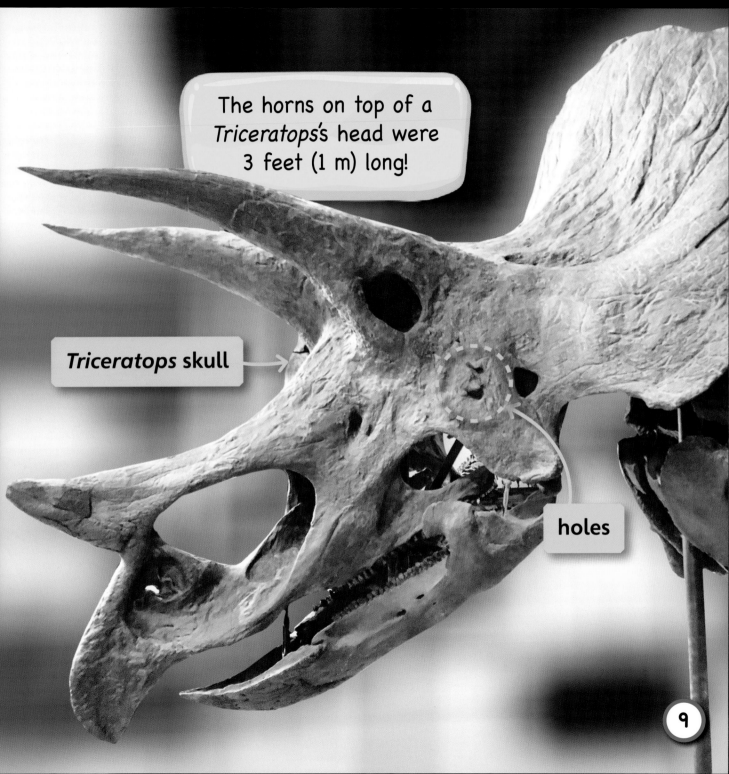

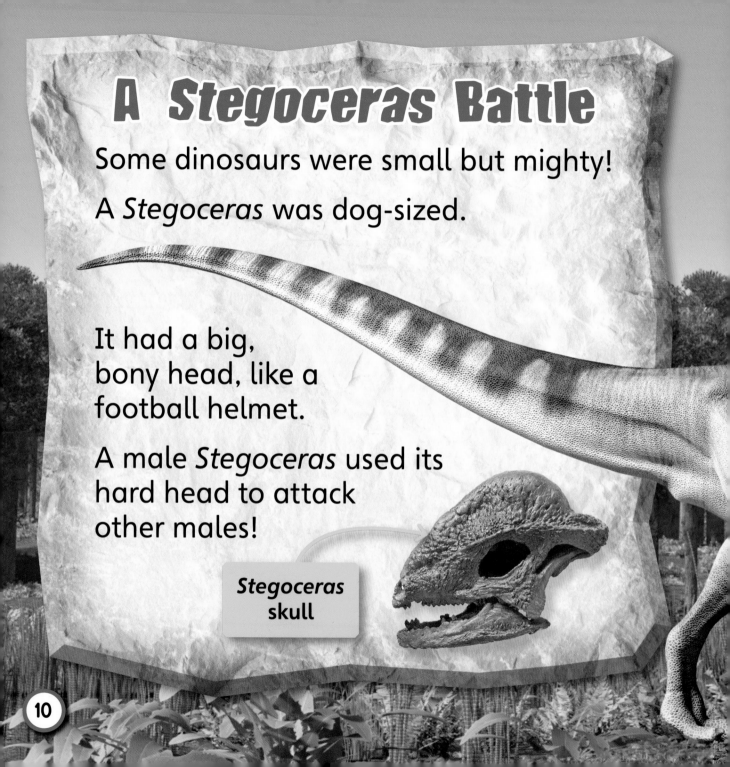

A *Stegoceras* Battle

Some dinosaurs were small but mighty!

A *Stegoceras* was dog-sized.

It had a big, bony head, like a football helmet.

A male *Stegoceras* used its hard head to attack other males!

Stegoceras skull

Why did these dinosaurs fight? Scientists think they fought over females.

Stegoceras
(STEG-oh-ser-us)

Fighting with Spikes

Dinosaurs also fought to stay safe.

Stegosaurus fought off *Allosaurus* with its spiky tail.

Scientists found an *Allosaurus* fossil with a hole in it.

The hole matched the spike on the tail of a *Stegosaurus*!

Allosaurus
(AL-oh-sor-uhs)

A *Stegosaurus* had four spikes on its tail. Each spike was 3 feet (1 m) long.

Stegosaurus
(STEG-oh-sor-us)

13

A Big Bite

Tyrannosaurus rex, or *T. rex*, hunted for plant-eating dinosaurs.

One day, millions of years ago, a *T. rex* attacked an *Edmontosaurus*.

The *T. rex* took a bite from the plant-eater's tail.

How do we know?

The edges of a *T. rex's* teeth were **jagged** to slice through meat.

T. rex tooth

Tyrannosaurus rex
(ti-ran-uh-SOR-uhs REKS)

Edmontosaurus
(ED-mohn-tow-sor-uhs)

T. rex Warriors

Scientists found an *Edmontosaurus* tailbone fossil.

There's a broken *T. rex* tooth in the bone!

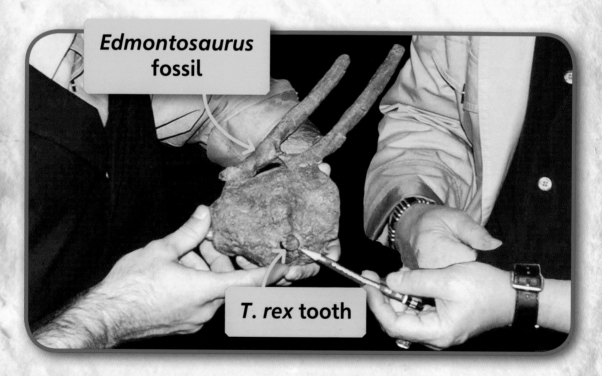

Edmontosaurus fossil

T. rex tooth

It shows that a *T. rex* attacked an *Edmontosaurus*.

Some *T. rex* skulls have *T. rex* tooth marks in them. *T. rexes* fought each other, too!

T. rex skull

T. rex tooth marks

Food Fight!

Dinosaurs called *Deinonychuses* battled over food.

Deinonychus
(dye-NON-ih-kuss)

Scientists found fossils of large and small *Deinonychuses*.

They were fighting over meat.

The scientists discovered that the big ones killed and ate the smaller ones!

Komodo dragon

Today, lizards called Komodo dragons fight over food in the same way.

Fighting Forever

Scientists found a fossil of two dinosaurs locked together.

Long ago, a fierce *Velociraptor* attacked a *Protoceratops*.

The *Velociraptor's* foot claw stabbed the plant-eater's neck.

Then, the two dinosaurs died and were buried in sand.

Over time, their bodies turned to rock, trapping the fighters forever!

Protoceratops
(PRO-toe-ser-uh-tops)

Velociraptor
(vuh-LOSS-uh-rap-tawr)

Glossary

fossils (FOSS-uhlz) the rocky remains of animals and plants that lived millions of years ago

herd (HURD) a large group of animals that live together

jagged (JAG-id) having a rough edge made up of sharp points

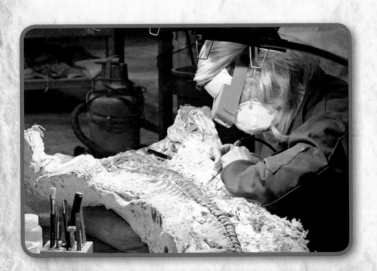

scientists (SYE-uhn-tists) people who study nature and the world

Index

Read More

Ganeri, Anita, and David West. *Dinosaurs (Monster Fight Club).* New York: Rosen (2012).

O'Hearn, Michael. *Triceratops vs. Stegosaurus: When Horns and Plates Collide (Dinosaur Wars).* North Mankato, MN: Capstone (2010).

Learn More Online

To learn more about dinosaurs, visit
www.bearportpublishing.com/dinosphere

About the Author

Ruth Owen has been developing and writing children's books for more than ten years. She first discovered dinosaurs when she was four years old—and loves them as much today as she did then!